Stefania is available for school visits, readings, author talks, book signings, and art sessions.
Virtual or in-person.
Contact her at:
sfmunzi@gmail.com
stefaniamuniz-logus.com

© 2021 Stefania Munzi-Logus. All rights reserved.

ISBN: 978-1-956159-10-3 (ebook)
978-1-956159-05-9 (print)

Edited by Sirah Jarocki. Book Design by Red Panda Editorial Services

Alphabet Publishing
1024 Main St. #172
Branford, CT 06405
USA
info@alphabetpublishingbooks.com
www.alphabetpublishingbooks.com

Jojo's Tiny Ear

Written and Illustrated by Stefania Munzi-Logus

Praise for Jojo's Tiny Ear

"A cute and fun easy-to-follow children's book. I love the fun rhymes along with the education about deafness." — Rikki Poynter

"…a powerful ode to the beauty of our differences and a memorable, uplifting lesson for kids about the importance of acceptance and kindness." — *BookLife*

"An enjoyable story of difference and acceptance" — *Kirkus Reviews*

"An upbeat, personalized picture book [that] encourages others to appreciate the seen and unseen differences between people." — *Foreword Reviews*

"I adored the story and the passion the author has put into her writing." — *Whispering Stories*

"a heartfelt book which celebrates a young boy born with a small ear. … illuminating for anyone not familiar with this condition." — Patty Lakin, author of *Dad and Me in the Morning*

"A wonderfully educational story that promotes acceptance, diversity, inclusion and being comfortable with who you are. This vibrant picture book will entertain as well as it educates" — *Literary Titans*

"This book would be perfect for a child that is just a little different… or who has a classmate or friend who is." — Jamie Jack, *Goodreads* reviewer

"Thank you for bringing awareness and understanding to facial differences and hearing loss. This beautifully illustrated children's book can help facilitate dialogue towards empathy and compassion." — Dr. Sheryl Lewin,

"This beautifully illustrated book shares a powerful message about how kids who have differences are typical kids. They want to be included and treated like any other kid." —Valli Gideons, author of *Now Hear This: Harper Soars with her Magic Ears*

"As someone who was born with microtia as well, it is important for stories like this one to introduce children and families to the specifics associated with the condition." — Dr. Justine Green, author of *Completely* Me

"an inspiring and sweet story…told in rhyming verse and accompanied by bright, colorful illustrations, this heartwarming story [is] Beautifully told." Emily-Jane Hills Orford, *Readers' Favorite*

"… a must read for parents teaching their children about empathy and compassion." — Victoria Irwin, *Reedsy's Discovery*

"I also have a child with microtia and I was very excited to purchase this book. The illustrations and story line are wonderful. I have followed the author/illustrator on social media and have watched a lot of interviews with her and I think she is amazing. Her own personal story is very inspiring and gives me hope.." — Judy1990, Amazon buyer

"The fact that it highlights we are all unique sends a simple, but strong message that while each of us are different we all share the same challenges in life – albeit in different ways and that each obstacle can be overcome with each incremental step! This story book for young children encapsulates that very essence – I know this – for I am deaf, too." — Carl Morris, World Pool Champion

Here comes Jojo.
He's a happy little boy.
He plays with his car.
It is his favorite toy.

Jojo can do anything, just like you.
He loves his pets.
He plays with them too.

Jojo likes the swings at the park.
He likes going to the zoo.
He likes watching fireworks in the dark.
There are many things he loves to do.

Jojo can travel to a far off place.
His mommy packs his favorite things.
The beauty brings a smile to his face.

Jojo is a happy little boy.
This is clear,
But he has one small difference:
Jojo has one tiny ear.

When Jojo was born, one ear did not grow.
It stayed small.
His ear was so tiny, no sound entered at all.

Jojo needs a hearing aid for his tiny ear.
It looks a little different,
But it makes the world more clear.

The hearing aid goes on a band that wraps around his head.
It has a shaky piece called a BAHA
that helps the sound to spread.

One day while Jojo was on the playground,
Two boys pushed him in the sand.
They asked him a tough question as they scowled,
"If you are a boy, why are you wearing a headband?"

This was something Jojo had never thought of.
His headband was bright, and what's more,
It had pictures of the things that he loved:
Cars, trucks, balls, and dinosaurs.

At first Jojo was very sad, and he did not understand.
Why were these two boys so mean?
Why did they hate his headband?

Then Jojo realized they might never have seen a tiny ear.
Maybe he needed to teach them about his headband
And how it made sound clear.

If you've never seen a tiny ear, that's OK.
Jojo's tiny ear makes him special and strong.
He will show off his tiny ear any day.
Though his ear is different, there is nothing wrong.

People don't always understand the tiny ear.
When they're confused, Jojo smiles and says,
"I have one small ear. I wear a hearing aid to help it hear."

If Jojo cannot hear you the first time.
Please be patient with the time it took.
Do not roll your eyes and say, "Never mind."
Listening with a tiny ear can be harder than it looks.

If you want to help Jojo's tiny ear hear the best,
Do not cover your mouth or turn your back.
This will help your words be more clear than the rest.

Sign language is a way Jojo speaks too.
There are no voiced sounds,
Just silent hand motions that speak to you.

Jojo knows sign language for the word "play."
He loves to run and jump.
The boys asked, "Can you go outside?"
Jojo said, "Of course, I go out every day."

Jojo takes his tiny ear to the beach.
He can hear the sound of the waves
He can hear beautiful songs and speech.
He still laughs and plays for all his happy days.

Jojo plays in the water.
He has his own little pool.
Blue is his favorite color.
He has lots of friends at school

Jojo loves to read books.
He plays football with Daddy too.
He helps when Mommy cooks.
He likes to have fun, just like you.

Everyone in the world is unique
We all have differences. It's not bad.
Some kids need glasses or tools to
help them speak.
Without our
individuality, the
world would
be sad.

Do not get discouraged if you are different.
Though the challenges may seem great.
You matter because you are brilliant.
You are wanted. Go out and create.

Be proud of what makes you, you.
We all thrive with our own technique.
You are valuable too.
The world is more beautiful when we are all unique.

Made in the USA
Las Vegas, NV
22 February 2022